THE NICK OF TIME

THE NICK OF TIME

JOHN LEVETT

Shoestring Press

Printed by imprintdigital
Upton Pyne, Exeter
www.imprintdigital.net

Typeset by narrator
www.narrator.me.uk
info@narrator.me.uk
033 022 300 39

Published by Shoestring Press
19 Devonshire Avenue, Beeston, Nottingham, NG9 1BS
(0115) 925 1827
www.shoestringpress.co.uk

First published 2014

ISBN 978 1 910323 10 6

ACKNOWLEDGEMENTS

Grateful acknowledgement are made to the following, in which some of these poems first appeared:

Critcal Quarterly, London Magazine, Magma, Poetry Durham, The Kent & Sussex Poetry Society Anthology 2009, The Interpreter's House, The Reader, The Spectator, The Times Literary Supplement and The Warwick Review.

For Wendy

CONTENTS

THE ICE HOUSE

A touch of Brunelleschi in its dome
        Glimpsed through the trees
Intrigued us just enough to cross the stream
And enter, through its map of yellow moss,
A culture that pre-dated CFCs
And died out with the big house years ago
To leave this lichened symbol of its loss
Washed over by new money's undertow.

Its trashed now, full of rubble, silver tins,
        Chunked styrofoam
And puddles growing ice like second skins
As we climb down a hundred years too late
To shiver underneath its brick-lined dome
Not daring to turn round or test the floor
And shocked at how the rich can insulate
Their world against the cold hands of the poor.

Each step is a cut passage through the years
        To rush us past
Lost generations, glacial chandeliers,
Their drops of sunlight dangling in the rain
As slow melt-water, loosening at last,
Wells up through alder, ash and sycamore
And leaves the breathless ghosts of ice to drain
Down through the rubbish piled against the door.

Go down once more, go back into the dark
          And hack into
The frozen heart of money's landscaped park,
Exhume old light, release its bubbled air
And feel your lips and fingers turning blue
Then cart it back and watch exhaustion pass
In candlelight through crystal as you stare
At all your labour chiming in a glass.

THE HOLLY LEAF

For months she'd watched its glossy green
Begin to mottle, blotch and fade
Then thin to rigging winds picked clean,
Warm breezes fussily crocheted,
Snagged on a shrub, hung out to dry
Cat's-cradled by a cobweb, blown
From inside out to calcify
On weed-cracked crazy paving stone,
Until, snared by white plastering,
Still trying to give earth the slip,
With yellow gloves it entered spring
Between her thumb and fingertip.

She'd left it on the kitchen sill
To bleach with J-cloths in the sun,
Watched autumn gauzily unveil,
Headlamps strip-search its skeleton;
A peek into an afterlife
As beauty, ceasing to exist,
Still goes on looking for itself,
Becomes its own anatomist,
Lays bare the damage, lets her heart
Respond again to what love asks
Between electrodes that jump-start
Its journey back through tube and mask

Then leaves her drifting in the ward,
The night-light like a cold blue star
Above her silver bed's clipboard,
Its graphs, its felt-tipped DNR.
We cleaned and hoovered, placed the leaf
Reflectively on stainless steel,

A gift, a charm against our grief
To catch her spirit by the heel
As, moving round an empty house,
It tries each closed glass panelled door
And, weightless in the polished hush,
Slips through them like a conjuror.

DOUBLE YELLOW

This street was birdsong once and land
stripped back, ploughed up like caramel
where barley sprouted, silence fell
through ears and husks a sea-wind fanned,
and where once toadflax, willowherb,
or honeysuckle fringed the field,
where dew and cuckoo spit distilled,
two yellow lines now track the kerb,
as though these off-cuts from the sun
boiled down to strips in black asphalt
had lost in tightening green belt
their neolithic power to stun,
and settled, an ironic twist,
into this *cordon sanitaire*
to meet the carbonizing glare
of the lost and goaded motorist.

In place of bailed and stacked-up hay
an air-conditioned precinct looms
with atriums and catacombs
where downloads ambiently play.
Its microclimate towers and shuns
the warmth that pools beyond its glass,
like urine in an underpass
along its gutters sunshine runs,
and more than sunshine, more than heat,
more than the traffic warden knows
of orange cones and contraflows
is stacked-up underneath the street,
where, looking for a place to park
and passing yellow Hazchem signs

with plastic drains, downpipes that whine
of fossil fuels and toxic dark,
reluctant still to break the law,
I follow every turn and drop
then find the place, come to a stop,
and cool like some stalled Minotaur.

£1 an hour. We take the lift
and ping up past a dozen floors
then glimpse through automatic doors
the moon begin its cloudy shift,
and hear, as neon makes us blink,
blackbirds exorbitantly sing
deep in a checkout's chink-chink-chink
of earth and its slow vanishing.

WITNESS APPEAL

So many roadside shrines
With names and cellophaned bouquets
Our A-Zs and SatNavs cannot find
Left on grass banks or tied to Give Way signs;
Roses, freesias, tulips, marigolds
Placed near hard shoulders, lay-bys, asphalt splays,
By junctions and sliproads
To delicately hold
What time and its resurfacing erodes
In the buffeting and fumes we leave behind.

An unofficial grief
Is tissue-wrapped and temporized
As heavy rush-hour traffic rumbles past,
Its new blackspots confounding disbelief
With bordered cards, white candles lit in jars,
Frail tributes shock reflexively devised
Then reverently placed
To slow our passing cars,
To prove somehow that death can be outfaced
And love, in bleak tenacity, will last;

And so for some it must
But for the rest of us it fades
In fog as yellow Gatsos loom through mist
Or speed guns follow blue clouds of exhaust
And winters lace black tar with blacker ice.
Last spring I saw a poppyfield cascade
Towards a lane potholed
And coned off by police
As someone somewhere waited, unconsoled,
While dusk came down unnoticed, calls were missed.

It could be me today
Sent skidding though torrential rain
Past queues and temporary traffic lights
That line the route to one more RTA,
And all the cat's-eyes, all the contraflows,
All of grief's makeshift floral chicane
Lead to a metal sign
Where heavy traffic slows
As headlamps catch its yellows to outshine
A roadside jar of Winter aconites.

SEXING SKELETONS

The long bones and the pelvis are our clues
Now flesh is an abstraction, now the skin,
The coloured eye, the philtrum, lips and nose
Shrink back to leave just teeth stuck in the grin.

We mix-and-match them, pair them up to find
Who goes with who in this new afterlife,
And so long dead they surely will not mind;
We sort the bones for husband, bones for wife,

Their skulls, their jaws dropped open for old wine
Or maggots in dead tongues that wagged to prize
The sexiness of talus, sternum, spine
Time strips and agricultures pulverize.

We catalogue them, lay them side by side,
The disarticulated made to stir,
To find, deep in their carbon, ossified,
This bias for the male we disinter.

So even dead some women, second best,
Are dug up, disassembled, reassigned
And rattled by each wrong, bone-headed guess
Amongst the ribs and hips they leave behind.

Our x-rays catch them as they incandesce,
Stripped bare, irradiated, cheated twice,
Now light years from the rags of their last dress
And held up to the lamp in sacrifice.

GLITTERBALL

He'd worked the Transatlantic Room,
pinball machines on an iron-legged pier
that stuck out into the sixties
before its chained-up scrap-heap crashed
down through each pile to a column inch
at the murky foot of a front-page splash.
His element was chromium,
bent copper, nickel, milled half-crowns,
and neon in its early days,
its blink, its cranked-up flicker
drained in a fish-eye mirror
with cranes and a rusty dredger's
electroplated moon.

His life was beer, cheroots, fresh whelks,
black oysters from the ferrous tides,
their pubs and dives, their mother-of-pearl,
and the torchlit gleam as nets of eels
fetched up by an estuary
where diamond geezers kept their cool
and life went round like a glitterball.

Nowadays it's a hole-in-the-wall
where you swipe enough cash to get rat-arsed
then head for a club or a takeaway
and chicken-wire jackets his tidal bones
with their clack of shells, their gold toothpick,
their pockets of change in a crushed cape of shrimp.
Ask him now what became of it all
and he'll tip the metal plate in his skull
with its sunken cheeks, its stubble of moss,
its cradle-cap of phosphorous,

and swear the only brass he's seen
is the drowned girl picked skinnier every year,
and that something more than a battery lick
runs through the tails of the curious eels
since the money went electric.

DOLL

She begged for change down by the ferry gate,
The little girl her parents once extolled,
A tin of Carlsberg tipped to lubricate
The lick and spit in every fag she rolled.

She'd worked the pubs on pills, high as a kite,
Or talkative on Strongbow spiked with rain,
Humped Satan once as, pinpointing midnight,
The Dog Star, frozen, dangled from a crane.

Those voices in her head were all old mates
Who followed her to every place she kipped
Through brownfield sites, industrial estates
Barbed wire and halogen bled white and stripped.

They fished her from the dock, a dead cell phone
Flipped ready for her next soliloquy,
Her trolley bent and broken, her jawbone
Lolled open for a chinwag with the sea.

THE TOWER

St Peter & St Paul, Cromer

The last flight on our helical way
Is a brick and ropework tourniquet
That twists her shoulders as we rise
With spiralled steps fears somatize
While panic scrabbles, leaves a past
Sloughed backwards in its dried worm-cast,
Atavistic, pagan, caught
In postures old beliefs distort
And where, while spiders hesitate,
Dust floats down as a counterweight
To medieval turns that grace
The interstitial warp of space;
A journey up, an airless spin
Through horror's fossil origin,
Anomic, feeble, still enticed
By notions that, through God and Christ,
Salvation is, after the Fall,
Both circular and vertical.
We reach the end and as we're shucked
Out of the rooftop's lead-lined duct
She weighs up, high above the town,
The merits of the quick way down
Then hoicks her badged rucksack to show
That goose bumps, jitters, vertigo
Come jumbled with old socks and boots
One final shrug redistributes
To leave a tiny bird displayed
In henna on her shoulderblade,
Its blue wings wrinkling in mid-flight
Through two red welts brass buckles bite.

CLAVICLE

It was the only bone he ever broke,
    The slender one they can't repair
    That's left to slowly knit itself,
A made-to-measure bone, almost bespoke
    And ready with smashed vertebrae,
    Maxilla, carpals, ribs and roots
To turn up in a bulldozed cemetery
Brushed off and fingered, lifted like a flute
And played so sweetly not even a bird
Could match the melodies it disinterred
With thorn and briar and, coming up for air,
Its chill released, a sigh's diminished twelfth.

At first he was OK, disposed to rest
    He watched old movies on TV
    Or Busby Berkeley musicals
But affectless and idling, grew depressed,
    Imprisoned in his plumped-up bed
    Sunk deep inside their sheltered flat
Where, piling up behind the things unsaid,
Were boxes of Stilnoct and Seroxat;
Addicted, as though dentures hid a truth,
To sugars in the shell of his sweet tooth
And leaving, with missed pills and stone cold tea,
White moulded plastic trays of Ready Meals.

In dreams he cuts a dash, his polished shoes
    Tap dancing with top hat and cane
    Down glacial stairs into a room
Where moonlight and a silver TV fuse,
    Where in the underlit small hours
    And soft-shoe shuffling through a past
His tubed-up figure ghosts and dissappears
Somewhere between the brightness and contrast;
Caught by an x-ray days after his fall
He dances on with bones made visible,
Still in the dark, still miming to explain
The awkward shape his brilliant ribs assume.

WATER BOATMAN

A connoisseur of cooling surface tension
And all the polished ways a cloudscape flows,
He stops and brings your senses to attention,
Then tenses, walks away on glass tiptoes,

Or hangs and, upside down, collects a bubble,
Descending in its silvery membrane,
To plumb the depths and, like a spirit level,
Bob up into stability again.

When autumn and refraction make days shorter
He gathers dusk around him like a shawl
Then tips a battered moon into the water
To prove the garden pond unspillable.

He snatches your miraculous affection
With ways to sink or swim and lets you choose
To step out under stars from your reflection
And walk on water wearing his glass shoes.

PAPERWEIGHT

A cold spring sunshine comes and goes
Sliced up by our Venetian blind
And in between it briefly snows.
We stare out of our window thrilled
With each delicious change of mind
And buoyant, airtight, vacuum-sealed.

So this is what it's like to be
A toy in someone else's life
With moving parts that think they're free,
Our faces pressed to blobs of glue,
An underwater man and wife
Looked down upon and deep into.

Who tips us up? Inverts our room
And snows us with these whites and golds
As aqueously we assume,
Suspended in the morning's glare,
That something like a future holds
Our endlessly recycled stare?

Our dreams are tidal and their sky
Sucked back into sleep's hinterland
Blows inside out to amplify
This silence that a touch might break.
A high wind with its blue glass hand
Turns up to give us one more shake.

HEAVY WEATHER

Spun into colour
On breath's liquid tether
And streamed through the hoop in her wand
They show her how mist
Can briefly exist
Deliquescent with meanings beyond
The pendulous flight
Of baubled sunlight,
The heliotropical spin
As blown gyroscopes
Of rainbowing soaps
Revolve, iridescently thin

To their ionized sheen
Of red, blue and green
While golds evanescently rise
And each bubble pops
In a tingle of drops
Her stretched fingertips vaporize.
Strong like her mother
In such heavy weather
She blinks as the prismatic haze,
Its beauty dispersed
In an atomized burst,
Absolves the damp hand it betrays.

GLACIER MINTS

A morbid immobility
Turned her into the sort of geographical feature
Sheet ice transmutes,
A glass terrain we all tip-toed around;
Her chair an intricate dead tree
And, clutched like roots,
Her gnarled hands sprouting frigidly,
Her lap a polar mound
Of misty wrappers smoothed out, sticky-backed,
That glistened like each blue-eyed cataract.

You entered though a scent of mint
And found yourself in a different weather system,
Breath visible
On cut glass in her gleaming living room
And carrying an arctic hint,
Confected chill
That washed her like an aquatint,
A frosted bloom
Suffusing every kidney spot and crease
Reflected in the mirrored mantlepiece.

On Sunday nights the TV was outstared
With tear ducts slowly leaking their glacial debris,
Her brittle jaw
Set firm as splintered sugar turned opaque
Surviving under snow-white hair
The muffled roar
As bergs of memory calved and sheared
And in their wake
Light ricocheted through frost to sting her eyes
And all our stone cold faces crystallized.

BEATRICE CENCI

Guido Reni 17th C
Original in Rome

She hung around our scullery,
Looked down on us from its damp plastered wall
And "wasn't bad for fifteen bob" he said.
She peered out into shade
Serenely waiting for sunlight to fall
With all the eerie patience of the dead
Who, picked up for a song,
Are sure it won't be long,
The afterlife has simply been delayed.

She smiles, looks over her shoulder
And murky now with olives, browns and creams
Stares out into an emptiness nonplussed
Through varnishes that crack
On tin-tacked canvas splitting at the seams,
Still shaping up to slip past lamplit dust,
Escape her time and name
And shimmy from the frame
Shake off loose flakes, step out and not look back.

Maybe that's why he picked her up
In Angel's junk shop eighty years ago
Appealing as she must have to his sense
Of beauty and fair play
With eyes that saw what he would never know
Through almond lids and puddled innocence,
Attentiveness just missed
By this late copyist,
A neck the clumsy brushstrokes still betray.

I've tucked her underneath my arm
In bubblewrap to insulate her spell,
Secured her with two bows of garden string
To bring her safely home
And if I could I'd bring him back as well
To play the holy fool again, to sing
And like some dusty saint
Release her from her paint
And dance behind her all the way to Rome.

FORMICA

Our prefab walls were white
Rectangles pressed and flat-packed by machine,
Our chairs a plastic composite,
Our tabletop a yellow melamine;
Our all-electric kitchen ultra-bright,
Each module heat-resistant, reinforced,
Our rented home now blessed
By all that could be polished and compressed,
Our blitzed and splintered past
Annealed and smoothed to last
Until the cold war's final holocaust.

My father loved the stuff,
Its feel and all the light it could contain,
Its plastic gloss, its bright and tough
New surfaces I couldn't chip or stain,
A fingered shine his orange cloth could buff
As if it were an ego to wipe clean,
While resin cast its spells
And moulded us these gleaming outer shells
That indistinctly caught
Reflections to distort
The dumb-show of our lives beneath their sheen.

Our yellow table stood
The test of time and, packed for each quick flit,
Followed us like sunlight through a wood
To dingy rooms a bulb or lampstand lit,
Shone through the dawns and dusks of my childhood
With tannin rings from stone-cold mugs of tea,
Saw dusty evenings fade
And filter through glass jars of marmalade
Where, glowing in preserve,
Peel hung like twists of nerve
Still shredded from the day's anxiety.

I use it now for post,
Dead biros, bulldog clips, a paperweight,
And if he comes it's as a host,
A revenant old resins insulate
And thermoset into this yellow ghost
Reflective under ink stains, blobs of glue,
And as my shadows drop
Onto this underpolished tabletop
To wipe off tea or wine
The blur before the shine
Is his offended spirit passing through.

STRAIGHT AND NARROW

Finding its level
a cool navigation
glides with the swans
and tangled green nylon,
stirring its midges
deep into evening
where wild honeysuckle
pilots its perfume
down the still reach
of the silent canal,
nudging a Coke tin
into thick shadow
with dog-ends and ring-pulls
and torn polythene.

This summer the water,
rainbowed with diesel,
bright enough now
to drown all melancholy,
is dreaming of where
it once meant to flow,
far away from the cut,
from the straight,
from the narrow,
to fall like a river,
loop and meander
out of its channel's
imprisoning spell,
trickling through limestone,
clay beds and marshes

down to sea-level's
alluvial swell,
splashing in shallows
with spray-cans and bottles,
anxious for waves
to turn over and spill
sip lids and cartons,
the wreck of a buggy,
a blue rubber flip-flop
aimlessly circling
the moon as it fishes
in pools to reveal
a wire shopping trolley
and, spokeless and shining,
the bent silver rim
of a bicycle wheel.

SHIP IN A BOTTLE

White thread through rigging does the trick,
A complicated web of string
And a steady hand through the bottleneck
Until each mast
And cotton sail
Is readied on its hinge or spring
And raised again for voyaging
Through hand-blown glass
Crossed spars impale
Breathed on and polished like a charm
His huge distorted hands becalm.

This was the ship in which he'd flee,
The one-way passage life postpones
Through vitreous waves in a cobalt sea
Taken at flood
To run with tides
Along hot coasts that poured red stones
In powder through his fingerbones
Or shone on mud
The estuary rides
Or, driven by winds to the West,
Woke with stars in a torn crows-nest.

Before too long the blown sails sagged,
Tarred rigging shrivelled in the sun
And the stars washed up in their glass were clagged
With drips of glue
That crystalized
And shaken out no longer burned
To shine and herald his return
Out of the blue
Dreams improvise.
The ship that took him there and back
Has turned to boot sale bric-à-brac

Someone has tidied up and thrust
High on a shelf and out of sight,
Sunk between shafts of sunshine and dust;
A ship of fools
That journey through
The wakefulness of a summer night
Where memory bleeds out into white
As moonlight spools
In tears of glue
And sadness seals its last vacuum
And hope dies in an airless room.

A SWEET TOOTH

A boxed meringue, his *homage* to bad taste,
Stares back across the tablecloth; a hoax,
A candy cerebellum neatly laced
With cream through which a glacé cherry pokes:
Its complex sugars, light as hollowed bone,
Evacuate their pockets of hot air
And multiply to fraudulently clone
One vanilla, one pink strawberry hemisphere.
Concealed behind discoloured cellophane
His frail affair broke up, a sweet collapse,
Her intricately brittle featherbrain
A box of scented debris, letters, snaps.
He hovered with the fossilizing ghost
Of stale perfection powdering his tongue,
Its falling in, its puff of pastel dust
Sucked back into the airways of his lung;
The oxygen, the mummifying cake,
That other life beyond the sell-by-date
Where, white with shock, the plastic mask opaque,
I watched his hollow face disintegrate.

IMPERIAL LEATHER

Although he's gone
She still can't wash her hands of him,
Can't miss the wet reflections in each tile
Or how he shone
Through steam that made the glass shelves swim
With cracked ceramic glimpses of his smile
And can't explain
Why, labelless, his cherished slip of soap
Still yellows on the porcelain
Decaying like some ghostly isotope.

He's there today
And as she dips one blue-veined wrist
And gathers lather in each wrinkled hand
Light starts to play
Inside his mirror's fume of mist
She's delicately come to understand:
She runs both taps
And hums and gently turns her thinning ring
And rinses it and thinks, perhaps,
"His slip of soap is slowly vanishing,

What will I do
When this, the very last of him,
Dissolves and leaves me finally alone?
Diminish too?
Stand sideways in the light and thin
To finely brushed and powdered skin and bone?"
The radio
Playing Bach and Schubert now till late
Is drowned out by the water's flow
As note by note the songs disintegrate.

Nothing will last
But while it does she watches him
Above the silver plug-chain in the sink.
Her past is past,
His life a tidemark round the rim
And love an old skin slowly turning pink.
She'll lose him soon,
Look up one night into a frosted pane
On which a paring of the moon
Will break and wash away in summer rain.

THE RED TENT

Three triangles of raspberry cane
Tied up by bits of string
Draped with red nylon made a crooked tent
That sizzled in the garden that July
To stiflingly contain
The thunder of a brewing argument
While heat, sucked into it
With static's hiss and spit,
Gave each spiteful inflection its own sting
As voices whined and hovered and let fly.

Things hotted up. I stayed inside
Where, almost innocent,
I felt sweat bead and trickle down my spine.
It sealed me off as love and guilt got real,
The stuff they'd always hide,
Dissolve in spirits, wash away with wine;
And when their blood was up
I felt the warmth corrupt,
Its air turned purple, thick with what was meant,
Like clouds of insects crushed to cochineal.

The tent was dumped, its canes, its nylon flare
Dismantled one hot night
As orange streetlamps sucked out all its red
And with it bled her colours from the world
Through fern and maidenhair,
Her lipstick, rouge and nail varnish all fled
Down fifty years or more
To this dark corridor,
A hospice ward, a bed, a tent of light
And tiny now, she lying in it, curled.

GREEN MAN

Pick a tree
And never face uphill
Unless you're sporting rubber boots,
But even then it means each pee
Creates a rill,
Warm tributaries through leaves and roots.
Stay dryer,
Look to the high ground, seek
A safer place to leak,
Aspire.

Problem was
That all the nettled hills
Ran wild with thorn and blackberry,
Were inaccessible because
Wicked spills
Of spikes and barbs entangled me
To throttle
Dry ditch and weed-choked rise
With gnats and oversize
Greenbottle.

To the wood
That would not let me pee
As well as lamentations send
This curse: let it be understood
It will be me
That summons gales to break or bend
Or both,
White owls to bolt and fly
Through storms to petrify
Your undergrowth.

A thousand years
From now new ghosts might see
How myth springs from incontinence
And how the steam from local beers
Weeps history;
The birches' torn, sun-shredded tents
Slashed under
As bluebells every spring
Make light of lightning
Or thunder.

OBSEQUIES

She hovers by an angel white as chalk
Then kneels in her red coat to tend his grave
And while she digs she shuts her eyes to talk
As though to an old man who's misbehaved.
I stare out of the window, cannot hear
This dressing down of some poor skeleton,
But what she says seems passionate, sincere,
While I, deaf like the dead, stand looking on
At all these mossed inscriptions that retrace
The stone stabilities of time and place
Remembering grey ashes poured from urns,
My father first, then mother, always late,
Their view a field of stars that slowly turns,
Their graves eternally approximate.

I envy her carved headstone and its power,
Her faithfulness on this bright Easter day,
A sense that someone dead can yet somehow
Become, sneaked in by love, a stowaway;
Curl up in scent still haunting an old scarf,
Slip in between a first and second glance,
Duck down behind themselves in photographs,
Leave body-heat where clouds of midges dance.
Elusive, solemn, shy, mischievious,
What's left of them goes living on in us,
And so today I'm glad that nothing much
Will pierce this mix of sunshine and exhaust
Or their everlasting silence that's a touch
Indignant now at what the coffins cost.

FUNERAL

The way his mirror speckled
On the anaglypta wall
Drew me to the gloom above
The depths through which we fall,
And the way in which, while falling,
We gather in decline
Accumulating sadnesses
Reflections undermine,

Distorted affirmations
Silvered to displace
The collagen collapsing
On the bones inside my face,
Astonished at the yearning
In its unfamiliar shape
Intricate with shadows
And their clamour to escape

The vanity that holds me
Floating under dust
Facing the pretension
A brand new grief has sussed.
You are, I hear dad whisper
From the narcissistic pool,
A copy of a copy of
A copy of a fool.

A LIVING STATUE

This is the life we'd never want,
Imprisoned by a stranger's blink
In silver paint from head to sandalled toe,
A minor nymph in some *tableau vivant;*
Her skin, no longer molten, stretched to show
How movement turns soft tissue to a chink
In armour that preserves her and protects
The rest of us from what might happen next.

She's stopped the world but not got off
And now the world starts up again
She's trapped inside her immobility,
A solipsist, an existential tough
Who, sacrificing freedom to be free,
Addresses money, staring out through rain
Into her pool of silver as we spill
Round puddles all her stillnesses distil.

She blanks the evening, tricks street light
And holds her catatonic pose
Immaculate and stylized and gone
Deep under cover, hiding in plain sight,
Or briefly jerks, a slim automaton
Towards an inwardness only she knows,
Till life comes sidling up to make a mess
Of all her poise and patient shininess.

I saw her once scrubbed up, dead clean
And almost motionless until
She turned and met my shock with her surprise
To let real life fleetingly intervene;
She blinked and smiled as though against her will
Betrayed by flecks of silver round her eyes
And lowered both her lids at my long stare
Like two spun coins suspended in mid-air.

TRIANGLE

A whitewashed wall
And wooden ladder painted black
Made up the triangle
Of cables, masts and rigging, harbour views
All framed by its sun-struck hypotenuse
Left angled to
Its 45° of white and blue
From which, it seemed, there was no turning back.

She took a breath
Then with crossed fingers closed her eyes
To blindly dodge beneath
And something in the taut way that she went
Seemed tentatively held to circumvent
Her fear, its weight
That made her orange T-shirt hesitate
And red, stuck in its spectrum, agonize.

When she emerged
Relief swept through her like a gale
As ancient sunlight surged
And shadow, like a skeleton that stole
Her beauty from inside the bone-white wall,
Somehow jumped clean
Out of its small three-sided world to mean
That everything that day would turn out well.

MOONLIGHT & ROSES

Red garage roses pass their sell-by-dates
Through yellow nights on forecourts in the rain
And, beaded by fluorescence, suffocate
With Baby's Breath in lungs of cellophane;

Above them, solvent still, old stars are milled
And scattered like Greek coins cast down for wine
Before the warm Aegean dark was spilled,
Loose silver foreign tongues dissolve and shine:

The small change of romance time flings away
To turn and sink through beams of halogen
Extinguishing the moon in each bouquet
Knocked out in cheap tin buckets for a song.

THE DEEP END

Two girls are slowly learning how to swim
                    In blue armbands
Inflated just enough to stay afloat,
Mouths shut against the chlorinated brim
          As doggedly and innocent
                    They frown and paddle hands
                    To where the teacher stands
And snorted water tightens in their throats;
          A month now since their father went
And left them treading water, heads held high,
Still trying hard to love, forgetting why.

The lawn is chained and scattered with wet leaves,
                    A yellowing
Reflected with sunshine in toughened glass
And shaken out as double-glazing heaves
          Their glitter over half the pool
                    To give last summer's bling
                    Its brilliant final fling
That sinks and shimmers through this morning's class.
          Blindsided by its dazzling fall
I try to blink away the bright membrane
Stretched over them like sunlit cellophane.

I wave and watch them dumbly semaphore
Knowing as they climb
Out of the pool to pad along wet tiles
They're not entirely my girls any more;
Reflectively they disappear,
Their grins, their hapless mime
Half in, half out of time
Absorbed by misted glass that reconciles
The deep end with a deeper fear
Condensing in me as I chill and wait
Like one long breath that won't evaporate.

UNDERSTUDY

Time, the scene-shifter, has done it again,
This sink and this mirror weren't here before,
Nor this old razor blade spotlit to explain
Her grubby white towel's arterial spoor,
As love, the scene-stealer, swans in from the wings,
Shaking a blisterpack, making a fist
Through a snowstorm of tissues pain numbingly flings
And wearing, like bangles, red cuts round her wrist.

The actor who played me is off, indisposed,
So, under-rehearsed, blood smeared on my hand,
I'm shoved on in a play I wrongly supposed
A light-hearted romance the critics had panned,
Waiting in rain for the fourth wall to break
With ambulance men at their curtain-calls
And the cock-eyed bow she's managed to take
And the hiss of wet tyres fading out like applause.

THE AFTERLIVES OF THE ANARCHISTS

Those staples in their foursquare silver strips
Stacked upward like some brutalist
Manhatten office block
Were teased apart by fingertips
And, jammed down in the stapler at half-cock,
Sent shockwaves up my wrist
Then pushed back in
They pierced the skin,
Refusing to align
With folded A4's creased and crooked spine.

Another bead of blood. Another botch.
Another pamphlet not quite straight
To join the dodgy pile,
Another squat for Special Branch to watch.
In those days no emoticons would smile,
No app would re-collate
The authors' rage
At each slipped page
As blood and bits of skin
Smeared Proudhon, Stirner, Goldman, Bakunin.

Still edgy and implacable they've gone
With smudges, thumbprints, films of dust,
Blurred ghosts that, hand-cranked, roll
From cyclostyle to silicon
Through purple aniline and methanol,
As digital exhaust
Shows they survive
In some hard drive
And, scanned, downloaded, binned,
Shrug off the world their staples underpinned.

GOING TO SEE THE WHALE

We were all going down to see the whale,
each one of us for a different reason
and everyone out of step with the other,
skirting the cliff-top Pay & Display
down to the dunes through Corsican pines,
down to the mottled pile of blubber
dead for five days
with its hacked-about mouth and rim of bubbles.

The sea was far out and the insular bay
was filled with circulating cagoules,
the silvery flash of camera phones
buffering things to an optical scale
and giving them a shine;
the mud, the sky, the massive whale
all backdrop to a dark unknown
frigid in the North wind's chill,
its faces, fixed or grinning, blown
into the iron-red cliff face,
the whale corpse still as stone.

We never made it, bottled out
and doubled back to the steep footpath
tailed by a monkish, shuffling crowd
in pull-cord hoods that had circled the dead
whale on the beach below.
Our's was an accusatory truth
the guilty sometimes stumble on;
shingle, sharp-edged, brushed from soles,
the wind's close shave with razor shells,
a bootprint's tell-tale waffle
of rubber-stamped reproof.

A DIFFERENCE OF OPINION

We can only imagine what a man thinks
When he's just lost his head on the guillotine
From the twenty or so of Lavoisier's blinks
And the thoughts, if any, he had in between;

A chance, as I feel the edge of her tongue
Sharp and ill-tempered go whispering by,
To blink from the basket and, bloodily swung,
Signal at last that we see eye to eye.

INCLUDED IN THE SALE

Its timbers warped,
The asphalt roof, rucked-up and paper thin
With tin-tacked edges, drops
To grimy windows where the skies begin,
Where, vegetating downward into heat,
The ivy and the Russian vine compete
With knots that crack
On frost and ice, on raffia and string,
On hessian that sacks
Upended terracotta's wintering
Till March, in yellow weeds, creeps through concrete
And lays its slabs of sunshine at our feet.

The warmth inside
Leaps for the open door, vaults hoes and rakes,
Stops short as it collides
With April winds that give tall trees the shakes
Then, circulating backward, joins the shade
That thickens in dry earth stuck on a spade.
What evening brings
Is more than just the drinking of daylight
By furred or see-through wings
Caught in the tensile spiders' web-strung night,
But calm and dark, a sign, a settlement
To show how well its resurrections went.

To pull it down
Would mean much more than loss or vacancy
Or clouds of midges drowned
In rain or mist or workmen's mugs of tea;
We know from re-wound film, despite the blur,
Things never quite go back to what they were.
So let it stand
A refuge now from lives we never meant,
A derelict, unplanned,
Lopsided and ramshackle covenant
With all that we come picking through the mess
In clumsy garden gloves to repossess.

THE GLORY OF KIEV

Another week of Soviet make-believe
As Europe held its breath and we exhaled
Three hundred thousand tons of chestnut leaves,
Blown, raked up and radiantly bailed

Then helicoptered out, their beauty ditched
And buried in contaminated zones,
Their catkins, transuranically enriched,
Irradiating frost and kulak bones.

Chernobyl showed us what the end might mean;
Sweet April, glowing round its graphite core,
Spewed radionuclides and iodine
And turned our nature tables nuclear.

Through starless nights, through showers of toxic rain,
We interred forests, polytunnelled fields,
Felled ash and birch, wrapped trunks in cellophane
And shovelled through black earth as it self-sealed;

The chestnuts swayed and shook in disbelief
At work that made our soldiers weep and choke
And grieved for every drift, each fallen leaf
Sent up without a single wisp of smoke.

BLUEBELL

Timing let you down
and spring's aggressive candour
pushed you on,
your daredevil blue
testing the air
in a misty, leaf-cut
sunbeam's flare.
Your rush to be a botanical star,
crushed by a frost, proved premature,
a two-day singularity
that wasn't the frailest, the bluest, the first
April has shrunk to slake its thirst.

Later, with the smokey blue they prized,
the mushroom-haunted woods were colonized
and mornings were a picnic for the thousands that came after
composing their cushions and pillows for summer,
for children lost in the breath-ghosted air
and the mists drinking their laughter.

SMALL CHANGE

A gentleman in a white mackintosh
Is tacking and zigzagging
Close to the edge,
Not drunk but perilously sloshed,
Held in a trance
As toy yachts weave
And midges dance
Down a sunbeam's sleeve
Until, with a shrug, his attention flagging,
He turns and stumbles, veers away
From his charmingly interrupted day,

Then slips down the tube with his oyster card
Picked up by CCTV
In the seconds before
He swans past the horrified guard;
His billowing mac
Thrown up like a rag
Dragged down the track
With his wallet and bag
Unzipped in the glare of the Jubilee
As luminous vests under the train
Still search for the odds and ends that remain.

Tomorrow this curve of white tunnelling
Will stir with convected speech
As tube after tube
Sucked in and out goes vacuuming
What's left of pain
With recycled air
Come round again
To find him there
Caught between sleepers, hands out to reach,
Along with the lost, the unconsoled,
The pocket of dark where his change has rolled.

THE POLYTHENE CHURCH

Now God has got a cheap sun-roof
To see the nave and chancel through,
A sheet to magnify the truth,
To amplify a hollow pew,
To peer into each sinner's soul
Like cat's eyes through a goldfish bowl.

We raise the roof each time we sing
And hear the bell-tower blow and flap
And stare out through the scaffolding
Where flesh and spirit overlap,
Trusting God knows what we mean
Through opaque waves of polythene.

Above it all the untouched spire
Soars up and takes its lightning rod
Into a world of ice and fire
Among the stars disciples trod,
While we all linger far below
To see which way the winds will blow.

Five hundred years of flint and brick
Are capped and lashed-up safely now
As architect and builder pick
Their ways between each grave and flower;
Two hard-hats sent to resurrect
What theft and disbelieving wrecked.

A red thermometer still shows
Just how much cash we need to make
To fix the leaks and overflows
And, rigged and shipshape, undertake
Our journey on a sea of debt
To Galilee and Olivet.

The church goes dark, its snuffed-out wicks
Confirm the night they smoke into
As winds prowl round each crucifix
And whistle up the bats that flew
Out of our belfry where, concussed,
A mute bell grows a tongue of dust,

And silence breaks us, makes us turn
To medieval vengeance, pray
For more than candlewax to burn
The men who took our roof away,
For Christ to lift up each thief's head
And God to pour the boiling lead.

THE PRICE WARS

Caught short just as the sun fan-blades
    Through shafts of building dust
To give their spectral colonnades
    A Greco-Roman thrust,

He wobbles out, slightly off-beam,
    The way wire trolleys go,
Astonished as gold pillars stream
    And, broken, fuse their glow

In columns of Ionic light
    That line each asphalt aisle
As cirrus opens to ignite
    A solar peristyle

Lit up behind this superstore
    Where, chased by radiance,
A troubled middle manager
    Unvelcro's for the Gents,

His hard hat bobbing past the bins,
    His bared white teeth fluoresced
Against the sunset furies in
    His orange safety vest;

Its tabs, its stencilled lettering,
    Its colour-coded glare,
Its hi-viz polyester zing
    Like red hot ironware,

Defensive, molten, losing shape
    And slowly catching fire
In flashes of reflective tape
    And diamonds of fusewire

That pinpoint him at dusk to shield
    What dazzles, what condemns,
The moon above the battlefield,
    The stars small stratagems,

The tabard of the warrior
    Who shakes it by the throat
And hangs it on the toilet door,
    A luminous turncoat.

RADIUM

Girls on the night shift, a luminous pose,
Their brushes of Undark licked to a point,
Glow through this negative, over-exposed
As nitrates turn their beauty back-to-front;
Their gestures and reversals are obscure,
Dim body counts, incinerating light,
Translucent features, laughter's spooky burr
Sunk into darkness, flaring inside-out.

It's too late now to catch the way things went,
Uranium has filleted the air,
Fluorescent jaws lit up with what was meant,
Lips turned candescant, tongues gone nuclear;
Absorbed in dials and minute-hands they trace
With brushstrokes what their radiance destroyed
As, freaked with paint, the grins that gut each face,
Outshining bones, burn through the celluloid.

FLY AWAY HOME

Hard to imagine them taking off,
their cardinal reds
so glossily encased,
their jet spots
so burnished.
Over-engineered
and under-powered
their wings unclasp,
vibrate like quartz,
their enamelling
too decorative for meaning,
their understated tooling
intricate with secrets
as they light out for an autumn
sealed off by double-glazing,
shining as they cluster
on a pane of frosted glass;
a brittle journey ended
on the wrong side of a future
suctioned to a window
September polished off
with streams of mites and aphids
refuelling in a sunbeam's
weightless exfiltration of its dust.

FLOC

I am the dog of Michel Gallimard
Who 54 years ago disappeared
Returning to tell you of how the soul flew
From the broken-necked body of Albert Camus
Head first from his seat to the back of the car
Past the wife and the daughter of poor Gallimard
Who, thrown in the air, both leapt for this soul
As he would have once at the mouth of his goal,
But came down hands empty beside the two men
Trapped in the Vega and dying in Sens.
All lay there and waited not knowing I knew
That the doctor arriving was Marcel Camus,
Too late for Albert but possessing the same
Strange, Sisyphian, Gallic surname.
Dazed they got up and staggered while I
Sniffing a mystery, unable to die
Limped off to worry, to puzzle, perplex
Obsessives inventing the things that came next
Under the plane trees, the plane trees of Sens
As the air turned to liquid, the liquid to bronze
While high overhead in the silence a bird
Was repeatedly trilling *absurd, absurd.*
I've run with this now for so many years
Through distortions of language and cameras and tears
But when I lit out the whole thing was a whim
As ghostly and insubstantial as film,
And yes, like a movie, a movie that starred
The vanishing dog of Michel Gallimard.

THE WIND FARM

This was the noise his future made,
isolate, hollow,
metronomic, hush-hush;
knocking-off carbon,
pick-pocketing air,
no finger or footprint,
no smoke, no fire.

Under their cowls the fan-blades thin
on laminate stalks so sharp they spin
at the meteorological drop of a pin.

This is the noise in his patched-up head
giant white blades go slicing through
as clouds in a cone of moonlit sky
blink open like an MRI
or Xerox bathing a military frown
in Millbank, Vauxhall, Porton Down.

Under their cowls the fan-blades chase
the moon down the track as its sleepers race
the sealed ghost train of nuclear waste.

Even this desolation is late.
No energy
but a price to pay
and red poppies in November:
Faslane, Greenham, Mildenhall
encrypted now beyond recall.
Today you're a culture, tomorrow toast.
Ghost nods to biometric ghost.

Under their cowls the fan-blades speak
through the mouth of the Thames with its cockney smirk
"Deterrence? Deterrence didn't work."

TOURBILLON

His glass door rings a bell
To open on a metronomic blare
Tick-tocking off the time that's still to come,
Old time that's gone and dropped in for repair
And time we cannot tell,
That's neither here nor there,
Inertial in a gleaming pendulum,
The quiet between each swing
That's almost deafening
Until our muffled voices break the spell.

How quick his second hands
Sweep up towards their oxidized deadline
Or scuttle round illuminated clocks
Like insects blackly clicking as they shine
On dials in marble stands
Whose workings undermine
The silence time perpetually unlocks,
Soft chimes and hollow ticks
That intricately mix
The bits and bobs of life he understands.

His gold escapements glide
Sunlit behind the window's bevelled glass
And float in twin reflections of my face
That watch me watching dusty seconds pass
As minutes re-arrive
In hairsprings, threads of brass
And balance wheels whose tiny movements chase
The child I almost knew
Around whom time once flew
For the quarter of an hour she was alive.

STYLUS

A thrush's piped song
gets stuck on a thorn
that picks out its whistle
lead-lined with moonlight
heart-piercingly caught
on ivy climbed through the hole in the wall,
where, a snail-track ago,
a fox with a fire in its tail slunk through,
and where now
dusk wells to fulfilment
round an oil-lamp and a smokey hollyhock.
Who could have known
that our spat in the sun
with its loose threads of rain,
its raffia-jacketed bottle of wine
on a sleeveless day propped at an easel would come
to such an astonished unravelling?
Drainings like this
run too quick and too deep for the colourist;
for violet to be indelibly fixed
or gentian never acrylicly stilled
is the failure of water, its spring-loaded brush:
or the night prove us wrong
with its hisses and scratches, our thin-tempered needle
that picks up the silver fox fur and the torn chickenwire,
balanced and scored on their fineness, a theme
in the thrush's occluded song.

THE NICK OF TIME

No sooner have the cuts dried on her arms
Than dawn begins to break
And light falls onto fingers it embalms
While blood that needs a blade to fly
Lies down inside her skin to die
And gives her soul a subcutaneous shake.

Propped up against smeared tiling for a pee
She phones them as it crawls
In purple slowly through each artery
And a heart that's tired of tube and drip
Recovers just enough to skip
Toward the morning's Roman numerals.

Another night got through, one more wet day
To look straight in the eyes
That swim up from her mirror and betray
The damage that she can't explain,
Her bloodshot head-to-head with pain,
The kick of slow-release SSRI's.

She lifts a glass to time, the nick of it
Then scores a deeper line
Still probing for a nerveless vein to slit
And as the two green men barge in
She feels their eyes rest on her skin
And knows this time she's cut it bloody fine.

KEYHOLE

She'd tell us, she said, for a lost pin's fee,
The fluke in a feather, a red lead balloon,
Green trimmings of fennel on mercury,
Orion itself and that zealot the moon
Loomed over August, cratered, opaque
And anxious at this peninsular pace
To catch what its silver scissorwork makes
Of the stonechats' black and white paperchase.
Meaning, we guessed, she'd not tell us at all,
Or not while these billowing clouds built a home
From sea moss and basalt, each cavity wall
Blown flocks and extruded adhesions of foam.
With dusk closing down and its birds on transmit
That very last evening, not wanting to leave,
She wrote our addresses, too complex to fit
On the scraps of newspaper she'd tucked up her sleeve,
Fished out, months later, from jumpers and bras
In a seaside bedsit with one good gas ring
And stuffed in the keyhole where, cold now as stars,
Not even the dead bothered listening.

GLASS CEILING

Skittering over wet gravel
ionized glints undermined
the moon on a high water table
dissolvingly silver-lined
black ice crazing on puddles
splintering under court shoes,
diffusing the steps she had taken
on the way she determined to lose.

Stealing through clinical darkness
not even the stars dispelled
she came in a wobble of torchlight
to banks where mud craters held
fragments of chalk like those tablets
she'd glassily hoarded to keep
for her short-sighted walk into water,
her broken appointment with sleep.

Trailing a necklace of bubbles,
as chilled out as she'd ever been,
she gazed at the water's glass ceiling
through algae and torn polythene
in weeds she'd pulled on turning over
with their hem-lines of midges and flies
tidied and fussed by the river
and dressed for a stranger's eyes.

ONE-ARMED BANDITS

i.m. D.P. 1950-2006

We were cutting the holly tree down to size,
Lopping the branches and scything off leaves
That pricked our fingers, poked our nest-stuffed eaves,
When you turned up, years early, struck like me
At how these thorn-pierced, berry-sprayed
Eighteen months of pagan shade
Had turned into three sacks of green debris.

Still whistling, on your way to lay a ghost,
You came and went on bursts of Classic Soul
In jeans and snake-belt, holly buttonhole.
Already now your bead of rain and blood
Had drained into these 50's snaps
Of us in pint-sized Pac-a-Macs
With grins bathed in the pier's pink neon flood.

Old copper blacked our fingers, weighed our hands,
Made holes in pockets, slipped through plastic chairs,
Held down the eyes of corpses in nightmares;
And so I wish you silver, things that ring,
Half crowns and shillings, chrome milk bars,
Old fruit machines to shake the stars
And the bright torrential sixpences they fling.

AURELIA

Gelatinous, lacking direction,
Lit up like they've gulped down a moon
Sucked under high tides in a harbour
Their glutinous night-lights festoon,
They are helpless in an aquarium
Where they bunch in a corner to die
Hydrostatically innocent
Of how they move or why.

So we float them in circular fish tanks
With a pump to push them around,
Blooming together and fusing
Like blips of ultrasound,
Their bioluminescence
And valve-adjusted flow
Turns water into moonshine
As they glide each undertow;

Languid and amniotic,
Throbbing as if they were free
To dream of a destination,
Elude a destiny.
Then one, powered down and drifting
In its ectoplasmic suit,
Comes billowing out of paradise
On a violet parachute,

Cold-shouldered by all the others,
Hung-up in its tideless sea
By a deeper, colloidal delusion,
A flounced translucency;
A spasm of alienation
That clenches on what it might mean
To extinguish the tear-filled brightness
In a pulse of gelatine.

A PHRENOLOGICAL HEAD

He's hung around the house for seven years,
        His cool ceramic bust
Looks Botox'd now, his brow and hollow crown
        Still keen to theorize
    Beneath a widow's peak of dust,
    But when the last light disappears
He apes concern, although he cannot frown,
        Disturbed perhaps that things
Have not gone quite as well as he had hoped
        And, though he has no eyes,
    Seems sensitive to how our books have coped
With all the damp a seventh autumn brings.

I found him in a garden centre sale
        Placed clinically beside
The tangled wiring of a silk bouquet
        Propped up by damaged gnomes,
    His cardboard label loosely tied
    Into a price-tagged pony tail
The breeze affectionately flicked away.
        His high gloss caught my eye,
The writing on his head that almost shone,
        And so I took him home
    But what I brought him back to then has gone
And he, tight-lipped, seems never to ask why.

Indifferent? Non-judgemental? I'm not sure.
        If he had half a mind
He'd want, I think, to keep me out of it,
        Stay mute, oracular.
    He follows things he cannot find,
    Rides out their shadows to explore
Dark corners into which he doesn't fit

And, sensing I'm not there,
Confronts a mirror shiningly outfaced
By lights from passing cars
Illuminating absence and displaced
By dawns and dusks that come to fill his stare.

Born out of commerce, error, pseudoscience,
He's lasted longer now
Than either you or I. Ubiquitous,
A conversation piece,
Surviving gaslight and steam-power
He offers up his empty glance
That goes on fleetingly reflecting us.
His shopfront on the Strand
Was full of lowered heads that, for a fee,
Found some sort of release
In knowing that, though pre-determined, he
Could give them back a life to understand.

We make up things. Our nonsense turns to dust.
The words on his bald head
Are old abstractions polished off by time;
The touch, the neural gaze
Mapping out his brain's false A-Z
Are holed up now inside a hollow bust
Our fingers ping to prove it doesn't chime.
He's not had a good press
And really all that's left is porcelain.
Forgive him his cracked glaze
And ask yourself, because he won't explain,
Just why there is no bump for Happiness.

CHEERS

Here's to the tide and the moon it's outworn
And here's to your jawline halfway through a yawn
And here's to the anglepoised North Norfolk coast
Keeping its flocked oystercatchers engrossed,

And here's to fresh Easterlies siphoning sand
From dunes hourglass weather has sifted and panned
For shells and sharp shingle across the sea floor
Our shadows move gingerly down to explore,

Bobbing about, playing tag with a sun
As it wrinkles the beach leaving mud underdone,
Or spilling, when cloud cover threatens their spree,
In soft corrugations between you and me,

And here's to their feathering, ruffled inside
Edgy white waves on the tip-tilted tide
That sip at cold ankles, tickle with salts
Your drinkable heelcups a morning exalts.